Let There be Order In th
Butler

All rights reserved. No part of this publication may be reproduced, distributed or transmitted in any form or by any means, including photocopying, recording, or other electronic or mechanical methods, without the prior written permission of the publisher,
except in the case of brief quotations embodied in critical reviews and certain other noncommercial uses permitted by copyright law. Although the author and publisher have made every effort to ensure that the information in this book was correct at press time, the author and publisher do not assume and hereby disclaim any liability to any party for any loss, damage, or disruption caused by
errors or omissions, whether such errors or omissions result from negligence, accident, or any other cause. Adherence to all applicable laws and regulations, including international, federal, state and local governing professional licensing, business practices, advertising, and all other aspects of doing business in the US, Canada or any other jurisdiction is the sole responsibility of the reader and consumer. Neither the author nor the publisher assumes any responsibility or liability whatsoever on behalf of the consumer or reader of this material. Any perceived slight of any
individual or organization is purely unintentional. The resources in this book are provided for informational purposes only and should not be used to replace the specialized training and professional judgment of a health care or mental health care professional.
Neither the author nor the publisher can be held responsible for the use of the information provided within this book. Please always consult a trained professional before making any decision regarding treatment of yourself or others.

For more information, email pastorrbutler@gmail.com.

TABLE OF CONTENTS

FOREWORD 3

Chapter One 11
CHRIST HAS ANNOUNCED HIMSELF

Chapter Two 19
YOU DON'T LOVE ME LIKE YOU USED TO

Chapter Three 27
WILLING TO GIVE YOUR LIVE

Chapter Four 33
KICK THE DEVIL OUT

Chapter Five 41
THE SCENT OF A WOMAN

Chapter Six 49
THE WALKING DEAD

Chapter Seven 65
IT'S ALL LOVE

Chapter Eight 89
OPEN THE DOOR

Chapter Nine 103
IN CONCLUSION

FOREWORD

It was a warm spring night almost 20 years. My friends Tiffany Larke, Darrell Nixon and Charles Mayhew asked me to come out to a service that was happening in Brooklyn, NY. Mayhew (a prophetic voice in his own right) was sponsoring a revival at this church in the Clinton Hill section of Brooklyn. If I'm honest, I really didn't feel like going to church this particular evening. But, on this platform on that night was a new acquaintance, Pastor Marquis Yearwood. Anyone who knows me knows that I've never been a huge fan of platform services. For the uninitiated, a "Platform Service" is a service where multiple preachers or speakers, expound on a thematic topic. Sometimes, they are given an over-arching theme that they all talk about. Sometimes, there are specific assigned topics from a theme. For me, having been in church my entire life, I had been to my fair share of these types of service and even preached at some. For me at that time (I'm ashamed to say), these types of services had become redundant and boring. "Platform" services had lost their luster (to me) and, I generally stayed away from them.

My entire reason for going on this night was to see my friends and hang out with them at the USA Diner in Queens afterward. That's what we did as church youth in the late 90's and early 2000's. We went to church, then went to eat afterwards. I decided within myself that I would go to be a support.... Afterall, it was "Passion Week" I should be in church, right?

I made my way from my apartment in East New York to Clinton Hill, parked outside the church and walked in. Not much longer after I had taken my seat, Pastor Yearwood walked in with another young man whom I had seen before but I didn't really know. Aside from

Yearwood, I didn't know who else was preaching that night.

As the service progressed, we worshipped, we prayed, we even danced but, now it was preaching time. In those days, if a preacher didn't show up the sponsor of the service had a couple of choices. They could either skip the missing person or they could get a replacement. Sometimes, if you were a preacher who just happened to be in the audience, you became the replacement. On this night, the decision was made to just skip the missing preacher. Pastor Yearwood got up and introduced the gentleman that came with him as the Pastor of Christian Community Baptist Church and, how hearing this preacher was going to be a treat. I rolled my eyes because, I mean, how many times had I heard that in a service like this and the person bombed. I mean, nuclear detonation. Was absolutely terrible. I sat back in my chair and waited for this preacher to get up and for his 7-10 minutes (standard platform timing for preachers) to be up.

I didn't realize it at that moment but, I was quite literally on a collision course with destiny that night.

PASTOR ROBERT VINCENT BUTLER II (Yes, I wrote it in all caps) stood behind that pulpit and proceeded to dissect the word of God with precision, passion, reverence and joy. The likes of which, I had never seen before, especially someone in my own generation! With the skill of a surgeon and, the dedication of a tactical master, Butler took us on a journey. I was mesmerized. It was quite literally in that moment that I realized that I had a ways to go both as a student of the word of God and as a preacher. But, Robert's preaching stirred up a desire in me that night, not to be the best preacher I could but, to become the most LEARNED preacher that I could be. I am forever grateful to him because, that night he challenged me to always get behind the pulpit with precision, passion reverence and, joy every time!

Those same qualities are evident in the work "LET THERE BE ORDER IN THE CHURCH". This manuscript captures the essence of God's heart toward his church. (Now) Bishop Butler dissects the churches of Asia Minor and relates them to the modern church age. This book Is written, not in the spirit of damnation or judgment but, as a love letter to us the people of God. "LET THERE BE ORDER IN THE CHURCH" serves as a textbook for Pentecostal, apostolic believers. A blueprint for finding and reverencing order in God's church.

The very first chapter reminds us through scripture and anecdote that ultimately, we serve a king who is not only to be loved but to be feared (reverenced).

One of my favorite passages in all of scripture is found In Revelation 3 where John writes about the "Key Of David". Bishop Butler skillfully walks us through what it means to have the key of David and, just exactly how the church should use those keys. Bishop Butler is not just an anointed orator and preacher but, he is also a learned man, holding a doctorate degree in theology. "LET THERE BE ORDER IN THE CHURCH" Is not just a passion project but, it is the dissertation of someone who understands the importance historically and prophetically of God's church.

Of all of the people that Bishop Butler could have chosen to write this foreword, I am humbled that he allowed me to be the one. He has no idea (well I guess he does now) how much he has inspired me. After that night in Brooklyn 20 years ago, I got the chance to officially meet him and since then, I am honored to call him my brother.

Whether you are curious about the 7 churches in the book of Revelation or, you are a pastor looking for a way to study and then teach your congregation about the status of the church. You may even be an Elder looking to grow your understanding of this subject, this book is a blueprint to help you understand the function and operation of God's church. LET THERE BE ORDER IN THE CHURCH!!!!

Humbly Submitted,
Bishop D. Elias Loadholt Sr.
Living Water Christian Center

DEDICATED TO

The Lords Church,
Where Jesus is Lord
The Church that's been established
by His Word
The Church that Love is building,
where the gates of hell shall not
prevail.
The Lords Church
Where Jesus is Lord.

Artell,
Kyle, Jeremiah, Kayla, Chynna,
Caelani
Mom, Dad
& Archbishop Eric R. Figueroa, Sr.

CHAPTER ONE
CHRIST HAS ANNOUNCED HIMSELF

I was in the spirit on the Lord's Day and heard behind me a great voice, as of a trumpet, saying I am Alpha and Omega, the first and the last:
Revelation 1: 10-11a

Reflecting on my childhood, I can recall playing with my siblings in the back room while my father was in the front of the apartment either cooking or listening to music. While we were in the back room, as with most siblings, our playing would turn into fighting. At the very moment that things got out of hand, my father's voice would emerge over all of the noise that was coming out of the back room. Once my father's voice was heard, all of the excitement in the room would come to a sudden stop. It was like his presence, even though we could not see him, was announced through his voice. There was power in the way he spoke and in the words he used. Without even seeing his face, we could tell exactly what daddy was feeling just from hearing his voice.

We are living in the day when the church is very loud. There is a lot going on in the church. Countless denominations and organizations are being established year after year, but the church's blatant disrespect of God's word remains unresolved. Today's church has lost focus of the important things. For example, we no longer look to the father for guidance. It is therefore safe to say that we don't trust the father like in times past. The word loud in Webster's dictionary is defined as obtrusive or offensive. Obtrusive means undesirably prominent and offensive means to cause displeasure or resentment. This is what God has been hearing from His church, obtrusive, undesirable noise. There is a worship song popular in today's church that says, "I love you Lord and I lift my voice, to worship you Oh my soul rejoice, take joy my King in what you hear, and let it be a sweet sound in your ear". After evaluating the way things are in the church, can we honestly say that we are producing the sweet sound of worship? Although our Music Ministries are the best on this side of Heaven, if we take the time to understand worship, we discover that worship is not in the songs we sing, nor is it in the way that we shout and dance, but rather in the way we dedicate our lives to the Master.

In the book of Revelation, the first chapter we hear The Lord Jesus announce himself like never before. John says, "I was in the spirit on the LORD'S DAY, and heard behind me a great voice, as of a Trumpet, saying, I am ALPHA and OMEGA, the FIRST and the LAST." Remember the voice I spoke of in the beginning of this chapter? Well this voice is very similar to that one, a great voice, as of a trumpet.

Historically, before the entrance of a King, the first thing you would hear is the announcement of His entry. You would then hear a member of the Kings Court say "All Hail the King." As the king would make his entry the trumpets would blast, and the king would begin to address his subjects. John announces in verse 7, "Behold, He cometh with clouds; and every eye shall see him:" He hears a great voice as of a trumpet and then turns to witness the entry of the King. When he turns, he has in his vision seven golden candlesticks which represent the seven churches of Asia Minor as well as the Complete Church. In the midst of the seven golden candlesticks the apostle saw the King. The King In the middle of the church is the Savior of the world. He is the GLORIFIED CHRIST, the Chief Shepherd. David writes in Psalm 24 "Lift up your heads, O ye gates; and be ye lift up, ye everlasting doors; and the King of Glory shall come in". I believe that the King of Glory has been trying to come into the church for some time now. However the church has lost her purpose and so the King of Glory stands outside like an unwanted guest. He watches, as we audaciously play church in his name. This is not to cast a shadow of judgment upon the church, but to highlight the large contrast between the operations of today's church and the church of old. They had power… we have good sounding choirs. Their men of God had integrity while some of us today can't even define integrity. There was a time when the church did not tolerate the things that are overlooked today. In the modern church it has become acceptable to preach and fornicate or cohabitate unwed. It has become a common practice to lead a less than exemplary life and still operate in leadership positions in the house of God. My friend, the devil is a liar. This is the reason why the church has lost her power, because we are busy preaching something but living nothing. It's time for the church, the body of Christ, to open our ears and listen for the announcement. We need to take our focus off of the things that are holding us back and put our focus on the will of God.

The vision of the church has been distorted because we have constantly ignored what the Lord is saying to the church. Not only have we ignored Him, but we have barred his entrance into the church. Here He is knocking at the door and we are too busy fulfilling our own agendas to answer his call. Study has proven that seven out of ten churches are visionless, which means that 70% of the church is dying because we refuse to hear what the spirit is saying to the church. Proverbs 29:18 says, "Where there is no vision, the people perish: but he that keepeth the law, happy is he." If we turn down our volume we will be able to hear, and when we hear the instructions we will then see the direction. (Hearing + Obedience = Revelation)

LET THERE BE ORDER IN THE CHURCH

CHAPTER TWO
YOU DON'T LOVE ME LIKE YOU USED TO

"Yet there is one thing wrong; you don't love me as at first! Think about those times of your first love (how different now!) and turn back to me again and work as you did before;
Rev. 2: 4–5a (TLB)

What would cause an individual to tell their loved one something like "you don't love me like you used to"? Evidently, for one to say such a thing they must have felt loved in the beginning of the relationship and as time passed on, the love began to deteriorate. The church is experiencing a similar phenomenon. We have become relaxed, and complacent. Much like the church of

Ephesus, we've let go of the love we once had. When we first got saved, no one could stop us from witnessing. When we first received Christ, no one could stop us from attending prayer meeting. However, we have become a comfortable church. We are content with just serving God on Sunday. We are content with our mediocre prayer lives. I remember a song my grandmother used to sing, "O Zion, what's the matter now? You don't pray like you used to pray, what's the matter now?" Well the answer to that question is simple, we don't love like we used to, we don't care like we used to, and we're not as interested anymore. John F. Walvoord identifies this characteristic as the cooling of the heart, which had overtaken the church of Ephesus in relationship to God. It was the dangerous forerunner of spiritual apathy which will eventually erase Christian testimony in stages. First, a cooling of spiritual love, then the love of God replaced by a love for the things of the world, followed by a departure from the faith and a loss of an effective spiritual testimony. This is because our attention has been drawn away from God. True love towards God is demonstrated through worship. Our worship, however, has been adulterated. We have contaminated the worship/love with a disease called contingency. This sickness is stripping the church of its power. Where we used to love God unconditionally, we now love him based on how far He lets us go. The church used to stand firm for holiness and now we are condoning and giving license to the cultural sin practices of the world, all to be more relatable and socially accepted. Watering down the unadulterated gospel and cry for holiness resulting in people leaving the worship service feeling good instead of changed. How can we love God when we won't do his will? Love is an action word, yet our actions are totally against the word of God. We won't even preach for free anymore. We as bishops, pastors, evangelists and teachers have put a price tag on gifts that we didn't pay to obtain, but we love God. That's not love. Love is when we decrease so that others might increase. Love is when we are willing to die so that someone else might live. Die in our finances so that someone would get saved when we preach the gospel. So now in Revelation 2 we hear the Lord say "I have this one thing against you." He acknowledges the fact that we maintain spiritual protocol by not allowing false teachers and false apostles to infiltrate the church. However He still has an issue with us and that issue is that He can no longer feel our love. He feels neglected. He doesn't feel like he can trust us to be there when he needs us.

There was a time when we would do everything we could to please God. But now so many things have become more important than Him. One might say, how could God say such a thing about me? Doesn't He see me attending church every Sunday? Doesn't He hear me singing praise to him? So why does he feel like I don't love him? When we hear the Lord ask Peter, "Do you love me?" Peter says yes, and so Jesus replies if you do then you'll "Feed my sheep." Let's consider the change in focal points mentioned in chapter one. With the high priority that's been placed on the politics of church, and with the "money-first" mentality adapted by the church, along with the "me-first" spirit in the pulpit, can we honestly conclude that the sheep are being fed? And if the church is guilty of not loving God, then who do we love? The Apostle Paul warned us in 2 Timothy 3:2 "For men shall be lovers of their own selves, covetous, boasters, proud, blasphemers, disobedient to parents, unthankful, unholy," This means that we love ourselves more than we love God and we love our things more than we love God. We ought not to love anything more than we love God, nor should we try to love Him equally as the other things in our lives. The Lord has referred to himself in scripture as a jealous God. He is stern when it comes to our love for Him. Exodus 34:14 says "You must worship no other gods but only the Lord, for He is a God who is passionate about his relationship with you." (NLT). At the close of this letter to this backslidden church (Revelation 2) he says "Look how far you have fallen from your first love! Turn back to me again and work as you did at first. If you don't, I will come and remove your lamp stand from its place among the churches." (NLT). We must have made him jealous of something because he has threatened to remove us from our place. This is not the first time we have heard God say that He will remove us, for in Deuteronomy 6:15 Moses declares "For the Lord your God, who lives among you, [walketh in the midst of the seven golden candlesticks] is a jealous God. His anger will flare up against you and wipe you from the face of the earth." (NLT). The time has come for us to turn back to real ministry, to regain the power that we once had because right now, all we have is a form of godliness, but we deny the power thereof. It is time to rekindle the flame that we once had: "and thou shalt love the Lord thy God with all thine heart, and with all thy soul, and with all thy might." Deuteronomy 6:5

Reference for Chapter 2:

Exodus 20:5
Exodus 34:14
Deuteronomy 4:24
Deuteronomy 5:9
Deuteronomy 6:5
Deuteronomy 6:15
Joshua 24:19
Matthew 22:3
Mark 12:30
John 21:16

CHAPTER THREE
WILLING TO GIVE YOUR LIFE

"I know thy works, and TRIBULATION, and poverty, (but thou art rich), and I know the blasphemy of them which say, they are Jews, and are not, but are the 'Synagogue of Satan'. Fear none of those things which thou shalt suffer: behold the devil shall cast some of you into prison, THAT YE MAY BE TRIED; and ye shall have tribulation ten days: be thou faithful UNTO death, and I will give you a CROWN OF LIFE.
Rev. 2:9-11 (KJV)

The church in its Ephesian period lost its first love, now in its Smyrna period the church is being asked how deep is your love? The root meaning for the word Smyrna is "bitterness", and it means "Myrrh", an ointment associated with DEATH. Now understand that the church is the body of Christ and in order for us to legitimately hold that title the church is subject to pass through the life experience of Christ. We must be willing to go through the storms that come our way, enduring tribulation, and being faithful unto death. Often times many are misled to believe that life as a Christian is a life without problems and circumstances, however, as the Apostle Paul writes to Timothy, (2 Tim 3:12) "Yea and all that will live godly in Christ Jesus shall suffer persecution."

Being saved does not exclude us from life's problems. Jesus, being the Christ, still faced temptation in the wilderness. Being tempted is not the sin, yielding to the temptation is the sin. For if we yield, how then can we present our bodies a living sacrifice? When we are tried in the fire of temptation, if we withstand the heat, we will come out as pure gold. Pause for a moment and think back on how many times the devil has tried to burn you with his fire, tempting you to sin and yet you were able to stand the test and not fall to the temptation of Satan. That's reason enough, to praise God. This is the perfect spot for a praise. If we refrain from falling, our bodies as a living sacrifice become more valuable when it is presented to God. The Lord says, "I know your poverty, (but thou art rich)." It sounds as if the lord is telling the church to stop looking at what we don't have and start looking at what we do have. Often times pastors and their church leaders become discouraged when they look around their ministry and begin identifying the things that they lack. Some fall into a state of depression while others resort to illegal activity in order to acquire what they deem necessary for success. All the church needs in order to survive is the power of the HOLY GHOST. It is desirable to have an abundance of finances, membership and partnerships, and while these are valuable assets to the ministry, they are not more valuable than the power and presence of God. If we have HIS PRESENCE we also have HIS PROVISION, and if we have HIS POWER there is nothing that we won't be able to POSSESS. "And I know the blasphemy of them which say, they are Jews, and are not, but are the 'Synagogue of Satan'." In other words, there are many who look like Christians, who talk like Christians, sing like and preach like Christians but at the end of the day they are not followers of Christ but rather are followers of Satan. They live multiple lives and serve multiple masters. The Lord says I know who is sitting in the midst of you, for though they wear the garment of praise (sheep clothing), they have contrite and evil spirits, they wish to stay in tradition never accepting change. In other words they move when they hear the music they like, but when the tune is changed to something unfamiliar to their liking, the wolf comes out of them. Fear none of those things which thou shalt suffer: what things? Ridicule, scornfulness, persecution, betrayal, being lied on, being talked about etc… For God hath not given us the spirit of fear, but of power, and of love, and of a sound mind. (2 Tim 1:7) The church is PRO-CHRIST, we stand for Christ and represent Christ therefore making us a target for anyone or anything that is ANTI-CHRIST. Beloved these are the last days and the devil is coming after us. We represent a Kingdom that he has been trying to destroy since his eviction from the presence of the Creator. We are a marked people. The devil doesn't search throughout his kingdom to determine whom he may devour, he already has them. He searches within our churches. He attacks our leaders and we SUFFER, he attacks our finances and we SUFFER, he attacks our homes and we SUFFER, Romans 8:17 says, "And if children, then heirs; heirs of God, and joint-heirs with Christ; if so be that we suffer with him, that we may be also glorified together."

CHAPTER FOUR
KICK THE DEVIL OUT

This is what you must write to the angel of the church in Pergamum: I am the one who has the sharp double-edged sword! Listen to what I say.
I know that you live where Satan has his throne. But you have kept true to my name. Right there where Satan lives, my faithful witness Antipas was taken from you and put to death. Even then you did not give up your faith in me. I do have a few things against you. Some of you are following the teaching of Balaam. Long ago he told Balak to teach the people of Israel to eat food that had been offered to idols and to be immoral. Now some of you are following the teaching of the Nicolaitans. Turn back! If you don't, I will come quickly and fight against these people. And my words will cut like a sword. If you have ears, listen to what the Spirit says to the churches. To everyone who wins the victory, I will give some of the hidden food. I will also give each one a white stone with a new name written on it. No one will know that name except the one who is given the stone.
Revelation 2:12-17 (CEV)

It is important for us to understand as Christian believers what SANCTIFICATION really is. It is

the act of being SET APART it is the act of being HOLY. Our church today however, has been the total opposite. We have tried so hard to fit into a system that our master never intended for us to be a part of. As time has passed we have become more like the world and less like the church of God. We have openly accepted the things of the world into the church. It is a sad analysis but I must admit that we have become equally yoked with unbelievers, and we have allowed the darkness of this corrupted world to become greater than the true light of holiness within the church. Christ opens this letter by saying, I am the one who has the sharp double-edged sword! Listen to what I say. This sword that Christ has represents his authority and his judgment. In other words " I am the one who has the authority over the church and who can judge the church.

I am the only one with the authority to judge. This statement has to be made because Christ wants to identify himself as the only authority and the only judge. Why? Because as long as Satan has a seat in our church, satan will always try to exalt himself above God. His seat in the church gives him the impression that he is in control of things, in control of our praise, in control of our worship, in control of our minds, in control of our lives.
2Co 6:14 Be ye not unequally yoked together with unbelievers: for what fellowship hath righteousness with unrighteousness? And what communion hath light with darkness?

The church of God is in a season where must take a stand against compromising. We cannot allow the enemy to enter into the body and manipulate us into believing that it is alright to accept the things of the world. They may offer us grant money, faith based money, and all kinds of secular support in an attempt to get us to believe that they have the best interest of the church at heart. Pastors and church Leaders be careful because this is a trick of the enemy. This world system that we live in is POWERED by money and if the world can inject their power into our churches they will then be able to tell us that we must do the things that will cause us to break the Laws of Holiness. This is a cry to church DON'T LET THE CHURCH BECOME SUBJECT TO THE WORLD. The church is the body of Christ and Christ cannot be subject to the world. Take a stand. Maintain the standards of holiness and kick the devil out.

Christ now begins to speak with a very stern tone. REPENT or I will come quickly and deal with you

appropriately with the sword in my mouth. He sounds like an annoyed Christ. He resembles the Christ who showed up in the temple and began to drive moneychangers and merchants out of the temple.
Mat 21:12-13 And Jesus went into the temple of God, and cast out all them that sold and bought in the temple, and overthrew the tables of the moneychangers, and the seats of them that sold doves, And said unto them, It is written, My house shall be called the house of prayer; but ye have made it a den of thieves. (KJV)

Notice how there is celebration and praise toward Christ. The entry into Jerusalem looks like a church service, and in the middle of the service that is given in His honor, his spirit becomes grieved. Luke 19:41 says, And when he was come near, he beheld the city, and wept over it. So grieved to the point that He stops the celebration and begins to clean house. He places judgment when He says, but ye have made it a den of thieves. This means that the church has become something that He never intended for her to become. We are guilty of making the devil comfortable in the church and this is because we don't want to be offensive to anyone. However, when you stand for holiness and righteousness it's not being offensive, it's being defensive, and you are contending for the faith. Jude 1:3-4 My dear friends, I really wanted to write you about God's saving power at work in our lives. But instead, I must write and ask you to defend the faith that God has once for all given to his people. Some godless people have sneaked in among us and are saying, "God treats us much better than we deserve, and so it is all right to be immoral." They even deny that we must obey Jesus Christ as our only Master and Lord. But long ago the Scriptures warned that these godless people were doomed. (CEV)

LET THERE BE ORDER IN THE CHURCH

CHAPTER FIVE
THE SCENT OF A WOMAN

And unto the angel of the church in Thyatira write; These things saith the Son of God, who hath his eyes like unto a flame of fire, and his feet are like fine brass; I know thy works, and charity, and service, and faith, and thy patience, and thy works; and the last to be more than the first. Notwithstanding I have a few things against thee, because thou sufferest that woman Jezebel, which calleth herself a prophetess, to teach and to seduce my servants to commit fornication, and to eat things sacrificed unto idols. And I gave her space to repent of her fornication; and she repented not.
Behold, I will cast her into a bed, and them that commit adultery with her into great tribulation, except they repent of their deeds.
Revelation 2:18-22 (KJV)

After delivering the letter to the believers at Pergamos, it is now time for the Lord to address the church in Thyatira. He opens this letter by commending the church for their works and charity and service and faith and again their works. This is quite a commendation. It is obvious that this church is a very charitable group of people who will go beyond the call of duty to prove that they are a working church. However, there is a major problem within this church and her name is Jezebel. The last time we hear this name Jezebel is in the Old Testament. She is the wife of Ahab, Daughter of Ethbaal. She is the one who tortures and kills the prophets of the Lord and she introduces pagan worship (the worship of Ba'al The sun god) to Israel. 1Kings 16th chapter.

Now she is not literally Jezebel. The Lord has named her according to her character. In other words, she has "The Spirit of Jezebel" or "The Scent of Jezebel" She has ushered the people of God into a state of Spiritual Adultery and Unfaithfulness to Him.

In the Old Testament when Ahab married Jezebel, she was able to persuade him to participate in Ba'al worship. She also convinced him to impose Ba'al worship on the people of Israel. Jezebel was persuasive and seductive. The worship of Ba'al allowed all sorts of carnal behavior. Not long after the people began to prefer the carnal, sensual worship of Ba'al. This has to be because there is a misinterpretation as it pertains to the Grace of God. God's Grace does not allow a compromise.

There are many false prophets who have the scent of Jezebel on them today. They have convinced many Ahab minded people (weak-willed individuals), that it is safe to continue worshipping Yahweh while incorporating the worship of other gods. Some of our churches are in danger of becoming a citadel or stronghold of idolatry and immorality. We have placed the One True God on an even ground with false gods. The clothes god, the materialistic god and the money god. Exodus 34:11-16 says; I will force out the Amorites, the Canaanites, the Hittites, the Perizzites, the Hivites, and the Jebusites, but you must do what I command you today. Don't make treaties with any of those people. If you do, it will be like falling into a trap. Instead, you must destroy their altars and tear down the sacred poles they use in the worship of the goddess Asherah. I demand your complete loyalty--you must not worship any other god! Don't make treaties with the people there, or you will soon find yourselves worshiping their gods and taking part in their sacrificial meals. Your men will even marry their women and be influenced to worship their gods. (Exodus 34:11-16 CEV)

Beloved, we are the Church of the Living God. The God who delivered His people out of Egypt. The God that our fathers trusted to feed them in the wilderness. HE ALONE is God and should not be subject to smell the scent of Jezebel on his Church. To the carnal minded person this scent is more like a perfume. However, to God it is a foul odor on the body. Hebrews 12:1 teaches us to "lay aside every weight and the sin" this weight of sin as caused and odor on the body. The spirit of Jezebel has caused many of us to partake in spiritual adultery and therefore we've become illegally intimate with other gods which has infected us with STD's (Spiritually Transmitted Diseases). These diseases have caused a foul odor on the body. God's Grace is not a license to sin. And many have practiced Polytheism because they feel that if you repent the graciousness of God will give you a pass. This is an erroneous doctrine and we as the twenty first century leader must guard the Lord's people from the spirit of Jezebel.

Richard Booker wrote in his book "The Overcomers" "The primary reason why the false prophetess was able to continue her disastrous teaching in the congregation at Thyatira was because the leadership was weak. When God calls people to a leadership role, He gives them an anointing and spiritual authority that equips them to serve. The leaders at Thyatira did not exercise their God-given authority to rebuke and correct the woman, and if necessary, cast her out of the congregation".

It is time for a cleansing. A Psalm 51:7 type of washing (Purge me with hyssop, and I shall be clean: wash me, and I shall be whiter than snow).

You think God does not know that we've been in an affair with Jezebel and her gods? When we come to be intimate with Him, her scent is still on us. When we invite Him to our places of worship her scent is still there. The Lord's message to the believers at Thyatira is so relevant to us today. The world is more anti-God than it has ever been. The choice to not compromise must be made. The spirit of Jezebel has risen and claims to speak for God.

1John 4:1(KJV) Beloved, believe not every spirit, but try the spirits whether they are of God: because many false prophets are gone out into the world.

1John 4:1(GW) Dear friends, don't believe all people who say that they have the Spirit. Instead, test them. See whether the spirit they have is from God, because there are many false prophets in the world.

It's time for us to REPENT and remove the stench of this idolatrous woman off of the Lord's church. For we are unto God a sweet savour of Christ,
(2 Corinthians 2:15a)

Stench: (A distinctive odor that is offensively unpleasant)

CHAPTER SIX
THE WALKING DEAD

And unto the angel of the church in Sardis write; These things saith he that hath the seven Spirits of God, and the seven stars; I know thy works, that thou hast a name that thou livest, and art dead. Be watchful, and strengthen the things which remain, that are ready to die: for I have not found thy works perfect before God. Remember therefore how thou hast received and heard, and hold fast, and repent. If therefore thou shalt not watch, I will come on thee as a thief, and thou shalt not know what hour I will come upon thee. Thou hast a few names even in Sardis which have not defiled their garments; and they shall walk with me in white: for they are worthy. He that overcometh, the same shall be clothed in white raiment; and I will not blot out his name out of the book of life, but I will confess his name before my Father, and before his angels. He that hath an ear, let him hear what the Spirit saith unto the churches.
(Revelation 3:1-6)

These things saith HE (Jesus) that hath the seven Spirits of God, and the seven stars;

Ever wonder about the seven Spirits before the throne of God (Rev. 1:4)? Or the seven Spirits of God possessed by Christ (Rev. 3:1)? Or the seven Spirits of God symbolized by the seven lamps of fire burning before the throne (Rev. 4:5)? Or the Lamb's seven eyes that are the seven Spirits of God (Rev. 5:6)? Here's the meaning.

According to Kevin Bauder of the Central Baptist Theological Seminary, the prophecy of the coming Messiah in Isaiah 11 begins with these words: Isa 11:1 And there shall come forth a rod out of the stem of Jesse, and a Branch shall grow out of his roots: Isa 11:2 And the spirit of the LORD shall rest upon him, the spirit of wisdom and understanding, the spirit of counsel and might, the spirit of knowledge and of the fear of the LORD;

That's a bunch of spirits. Count 'em.

I.   THE SPIRIT OF THE LORD (which should be the chief personality of the church).

Without HIM the church is dead.

II.   THE SPIRIT OF WISDOM (this wisdom is not just about knowing whats good for you, but applying that knowledge into your every day walk with God as a representative of the church).

Without HIM the church is dead.

III.   THE SPIRIT OF UNDERSTANDING (the spirit of understanding develops the gift of faith within us. Faith helps us to see the invisible. This kind of sight is essential to the life of the church).

Without HIM the church is dead.

IV. THE SPIRIT OF COUNSEL (this is how we receive direction and instruction, STRATEGIES for the mission of the church). Jesus said in John 16:13 "Howbeit when he, the Spirit of truth, is come, he will GUIDE you into all truth:"

Without HIM the church is dead.

V. THE SPIRIT OF STRENGTH (the POWER to DO what we the church have been instructed to do). Jesus said in Acts 1:8 But ye shall receive power, after that the Holy Ghost is come upon you: and ye shall be witnesses unto me both in Jerusalem, and in all Judaea, and in Samaria, and unto the uttermost part of the earth.

Without HIM the church is dead.

VI. The Spirit of knowledge (the word of knowledge is a spiritual gift listed in 1 Corinthians 12:8. It is associated with the ability to teach the faith, but also with forms of revelation similar to prophecy. It is closely related to another spiritual gift, the word of wisdom). For to one is given by the Spirit the word of wisdom; to another the word of knowledge by the same Spirit;

Without HIM the church is dead.

VII. The Spirit of the fear of the LORD The fear of the Lord is the beginning of knowledge…" (Proverbs 1:7). To gain worldly wisdom requires much effort, but to gain heavenly wisdom requires much SUBMISSION. "… put on the new man who is renewed in knowledge according to the image of Him who created him" (Colossians 3:10)

Without HIM the church is dead.

Of course, these are not seven distinct Spirits, but one Holy Spirit in His seven-fold activity. This passage probably refers to the theocratic anointing that characterized Old Testament figures who led the nation of Israel. Jesus Christ Messiah will possess this theocratic anointing in its fullness and perfection: the seven-fold Spirit of God.
THEOCRATIC: a form of government in which God and only God is recognized as the supreme civil ruler, God's laws being interpreted by the ecclesiastical authorities (earthen vessels).

Death: The event of dying or departure from life; the moment when life ends.

I know thy works, that thou hast a name that thou livest, and art dead

As we arrive at this fifth church, we find a people who are the epitome of having a FORM OF GODLINESS with no power. A ritualistic group of people who have prided themselves with their formality and prestige. They are the high sadity, uppity type of people who have become more impressed with the rich history of their church, the notable people who attend the church, the amount of money that church has, the properties that have been acquired, the degrees and the intellect of the people and so on and so on. However, with all these things representing LIFE, there is still something about them that causes the Lord to pronounce them DEAD. How can the church be DEAD? The church, which is a living organism, the church, which is the BODY of CHRIST, HOW CAN THE CHURCH BE DEAD? Very much like the church in Ephesus, the church in Sardis has lost the power of their outward witness to Christ. This church has known fame in the past but has now lost its glory. Politicians, Businessmen, Communities, Families and Nations at one point in time looked to us for guidance and direction. There was a day in time where we, the church of God was the most important institution known to society. At the time of this writing, Sardis was a city in ruins and the church was mirror image of the city. Boasting of its past glory and greatness, this church is guilty of living in a former season while trying to APPEAR ALIVE in the current times. This once great church was in decline and instead of developing a vision of progression, they opted to focus on the meaningless past in hopes of a resurgence of HOW THINGS USED TO BE. This is The Walking Dead Church. There's activity but there is no life. There is movement, but there is no breathing. This church is spiritually dead and in great need of RENEWAL and REVIVAL. Let us never forget that this is Jesus' church and if HIS church is dead, then it can be said that the church DOES NOT HAVE HIS SPIRIT.

John 6:63   It is the spirit that quickeneth; the flesh profiteth nothing: the words that I speak unto you, THEY ARE SPIRIT, AND THEY ARE LIFE.
Romans 8:10   And if Christ be in you, the body is dead because of sin;

BUT THE SPIRIT IS LIFE because of righteousness.
2Cor 3:6 Who also hath made us able ministers of the new testament; not of the letter, but of the spirit: for the letter killeth, BUT THE SPIRIT GIVETH LIFE.

So the question now is, if we are, in Jesus's opinion DEAD, as a result of not having HIS SPIRIT, but we appear to be ALIVE, then what spirit are we functioning with.

It is certainly time for us to check our spirit. We must open our hearts to a fresh outpouring of the Spirit of the Living God. Some may ask the question, how?

FIRST, we must BE WATCHFUL. On high alert. Paying attention to the gates. Warring in the spirit to fight off the approach and the attacks of the enemy. The devil is cunning. He will use whatever plots and schemes to fulfill his ultimate agenda, which is to KILL, STEAL and DESTROY. But Jesus the life giver of the church has come that we might have LIFE and have it more abundantly. We cannot and will not survive unless the congregation WAKE UP and WATCH as well as pray. The Apostle Paul wrote to the believers at Ephesus "Awake you who sleep, arise from the dead, and Christ will give you light". Ephesians 5:14

    SECOND, STRENGTHEN THE THINGS WHICH REMAIN, that are ready to die. Believe it or not, there is something left. But if we don't wake up and seek God for a fresh outpouring of HIS SPIRIT, the little spiritual life that remains will also die. We have forsaken God's Word and compromised our convictions. Fellowships, Reformations and

Denominations are slowly dying physically and spiritually and if we're not careful and WATCHFUL it wont be long before they are completely dead.

THIRD, REMEMBER THEREFORE HOW THOU HAST RECEIVED AND HEARD. As Christians we must reconnect with SOUND DOCTRINE. Preaching the word! In season and out of season. Convince, rebuke, exhort, with all longsuffering and teaching. For the time will come when they will not endure sound doctrine. 2 Timothy 4:2 If we do not get back to the basics of proclaiming the Word of God, which is God and was with God in the beginning (the foundation), then we will not be grounded in our faith, we will not be convicted of our sins, we wont be receptive to correction, and ultimately we will lose our witness. Dr. Richard Booker in his book The

Overcomers asked "Is this warning from the Lord relevant to us today? Unfortunately, the answer is yes! With the way seminaries teach future ministers that the Bible is not really the Word of God, that the miracles of Jesus are just "fairy tales," and that the Bible is an antiquated book written by men that is not relevant to our modern world. The result is that we will churches filled with people who don't hear the Word of God, don't know the Word of God, and don't believe the Word of God. This dead church can live again by the Word of God. 1 Peter 1:23 says "Being born again, not of corruptible seed, but of incorruptible, by the word of God, which liveth and abideth forever."

FOURTH, HOLD FAST. To Hold fast is to cling to something with all you might and refuse to let go. Hold fast to what? Hold fast to being watchful. Hold fast to strengthening what remains. Hold fast to proclaiming the unadulterated Word of God. Hold fast to your faith. Hold fast to His promise. Hold fast to Jesus. Seeing then that we have a great high priest, that is passed into the heavens, Jesus the Son of God, let us hold fast our profession. Hebrews 4:14

Let us hold fast the profession of our faith without wavering; (for he is faithful that promised;) Hebrews 10:23

FIFTH, REPENT. The hour of repentance has come to the church. We like the church at Sardis are plagued with a Religious Spirit instead of having the Holy Spirit. We have Dead Works and are void of Ministry. We preach sermons that make people feel good, instead of preaching and proclaiming the life changing Word of

God. We have the Form of Godliness but not the Function of Godliness. We are driven by Rituals and not Revival. We have plenty of Services but we're not Servicing. The Lord is calling us to REPENT. To turn away from the practices of the Dead Church and Live. Repent for mishandling Gods people. Repent for using the Word of God to gain an advantage over Gods people. REPENT and be forgiven.

And if my people who are called by my name become humble and pray, and look for me, AND TURN AWAY FROM THEIR EVIL WAYS, then I will hear them from heaven. I will forgive their sin and heal their land. (Cause them to LIVE)
2 Chronicles 7:14 (ERV)
The message to those in Sardis is that they had better quickly wake up to their deadly lethargy and watch out, because their salvation is in jeopardy.

Some theologians refer to Sardis as "the counterfeit church" because the LOOK ALIVE but are REALLY DEAD.

I close this chapter with the words of William Barclay in his book Letters to the Seven Churches, "a church is in danger of death when it begins to worship its own past… when it is more concerned with forms than with life… when it loves systems more than it loves Jesus Christ… when it is more concerned with material things above spiritual things".

CHAPTER SEVEN
IT'S ALL LOVE

"Write this to the angel of the church in Philadelphia: "Here is a message from the one who is holy and true, the one who holds the key of David. When he opens something, it cannot be closed. And when he closes something, it cannot be opened. "I know what you do. I have put before you an open door that no one can close. I know you are weak, but you have followed my teaching. You were not afraid to speak my name. Listen! There is a group that belongs to Satan. They say they are Jews, but they are liars. They are not true Jews. I will make them come before you and bow at your feet. They will know that you are the people I have loved. You followed my command to endure patiently. So I will keep you from the time of trouble that will come to the world—a time that will test everyone living on earth. "I am coming soon. Hold on to the faith you have, so that no one can take away your crown. Those who win the victory will be pillars in the temple of my God. I will make that happen for them. They will never again have to leave God's temple. I will write on them the name of my God and the name of the city of my God. That city is the new Jerusalem. It is coming down out of heaven from my God. I will also write my new name on them. Everyone who hears this should listen to what the Spirit says to the churches.
(Revelation 3:7-13)

There is no question about the meaning of the word Philadelphia. It means "Brotherly Love," and well describes the charity and brotherly fellowship that dissipated the bitter personal animosities that characterized the theological disputant of the "Sardis Period". Our previous church is pronounced DEAD and in need of a spiritual revival. A revival that would usher Gods presence back into His Church. A revival that would cause an outpouring resembling the day of Pentecost, a rebirthing of sorts since Pentecost is recognized as the birth of the church.

As I press toward the conclusion of this book, our world, in the year 2020 is experiencing a Global Pandemic due to COVID-19. Schools have been shut down, stores have been shut down, day to day life has been shut down and last but certainly not least, our churches have been closed in order to ensure safety. While quarantined, my home city of New York experienced a catastrophe like never before. The death of prominent Bishops and Pastors all over our city, shook our churches, families and communities to the point where the alarm clock of the kingdom has sounded, and we have been forced to arise from a slumber that most of us had no idea we were in. As a result, the church, I believe, has transitioned from her Sardis state (Dead Church State) to her Philadelphia state (A Favored Church) to a God Ordained season. Church, welcome to A GREAT AWAKENING. An AWAKENING that has Bishops, Pastors, Laity, and THE CHURCH as a whole and THE WORLD reconsidering the importance of

Relationship with God over Religion-ship and Ritualism.

Beloved, God wants to present His church as a church that is alive and faithful to Christ? A church that focuses upon Jesus Christ. A church that makes Jesus Christ the center of its ministries and activities. A church that focuses upon reaching and growing people for Christ. A church that focuses upon teaching people to love Christ and to love one another more and more. The church in Philadelphia represents the church that has returned back to the Word of God. Now in 2023, (yes, three years to complete this one chapter…lol), I believe God is REVIVING HIS CHURCH. After all that we have endured and encountered, revival has hit the church. We have had to adjust in a major way. How we do church has changed drastically. With attendance at an all time low, visual presentation must be top of the line in order to keep the attention of those who would rather watch the worship experience from home. However, there is a silver lining. We have indeed regained our focus; the internet has provided an avenue for evangelizing like never before. I personally, have been able to reach people across the globe simply by going live on Facebook, YouTube and all other social media platforms. This is a sort of REVIVAL. A REVIVAL in our commitment, a REVIVAL in our seriousness toward the things of God. A REVIVAL in our thought process as it pertains to the priorities of the business of the Kingdom. Let us celebrate this moment with the words of the great hymnologist W. P. Mackay:

We praise thee, O God, for the Son of thy love,
for Jesus who died, and is now gone above.
Hallelujah! Thine the glory, hallelujah! Amen!
Hallelujah! Thine the glory, REVIVE US AGAIN.

And unto the angel of the church in Philadelphia write; These things saith he that is holy, he that is true, he that hath the key of David.

HE THAT IS HOLY:
In this letter, Christ identifies Himself to the church as HOLY. It may sound cliché, but it will always remain a fact that HOLINESS IS RIGHT. There can be no order in the church without the mindset of holiness.

For I am the LORD your God: ye shall therefore sanctify yourselves, and YE SHALL BE HOLY;
FOR I AM HOLY: Leviticus 11:44

As we begin to do ministry in a post-pandemic era, we must adhere to the voice of the Lord and submit to holiness being the order of the day. We are called to be Christ-like. The representation of the character of Christ within the earth realm. A call to be Christ-like, is a call to holiness. HE THAT IS HOLY, wishes to position His church to be ready for the coming of the bridegroom.

HE THAT IS TRUE:
Jesus Christ is the One who is true. The word true (alethinos) means the true as opposed to the false, the genuine as opposed to the counterfeit, the real as opposed to the

unreal. Jesus Christ is the true, genuine, and real God. He is the only living and true God. There is none other. All the other gods worshipped by men are false, counterfeit, and unreal. This, too, means a wonderful thing. God is not far off in outer space someplace, too far off to be known or reached. He is not the shadowy figure that most men imagine Him to be. God is not distant from us. He has not left us in the dark to grope and grasp and to stumble about trying to find Him. God does not hate us; He has not left us in the dark about Himself. God loves us. He has revealed Himself to us. He sent the Lord Jesus Christ to bring the truth to us. Therefore, in worshipping the Lord Jesus Christ we are worshipping the only true and living God. What the faithful church must do is continue to follow Christ, continue to make Him the focus of all that it does. When the church makes Him the center of all its ministries, activities, and meetings, then the church is following the truth—following HE WHO IS TRUE. (From The Preachers Outline & Sermon Bible)

"That was the true Light, which lighteth every man that cometh into the world"
(John 1:9).

"And the Word was made flesh and dwelt among us, (and we beheld his glory, the glory as of the only begotten of the Father,) full of grace and TRUTH"
(John 1:14).

"Then Jesus said unto them, Verily, verily, I say unto you, Moses gave you not that bread from heaven; but my Father giveth you the TRUE bread from heaven" (John 6:32).

"Jesus saith unto him, I am the way, the TRUTH, and the life: no man cometh unto the Father, but by me" (John 14:6).

"I am the TRUE vine, and my Father is the husbandman" (John 15:1).

"Pilate therefore said unto him, Art thou a king then? Jesus answered, Thou sayest that I am a king. To this end was I born, and for this cause came I into the world, that I should bear witness unto the TRUTH. Every one that is of the
TRUTH heareth my voice"
(John. 18:37)

"Again, a new commandment I write unto you, which thing is TRUE in him and in you: because the darkness is past, and the TRUE light now shineth" (1 John 2:8)

HE THAT HATH THE KEY OF DAVID

I remember at the beginning of the pandemic I preached a message to our online audience "Give Me Back My Church". With sanctuaries closed to the public, and pastors having to figure out a way to stay connected to congregations, I realized that we were in position to become a better church. But first, some things needed to be changed. We were a church (the church as a whole) that was focused on the wrong things. God's church became a playground, and the quarantine was another version of Matthew 21:12 - 13

And Jesus went into the temple of God, and cast out all them that sold and bought in the temple, and overthrew the tables of the moneychangers, and the seats of them that sold doves,

And said unto them, It is written, My house shall be called the house of prayer; but ye have made it a den of thieves.

The keys that Christ gave to the church at Peter's confession gave us unlimited access to the earth realm and heavenly realm. And just like a parent, God had snatched our keys in order to regain CONTROL OF HIS CHURCH.
A key denotes authority, control, access, ownership; and the key of David is the throne that God promised to king David.
2 Samuel 7:12-13, 16;
12. And when thy days be fulfilled, and thou shalt sleep with thy fathers, I will set up thy seed after thee, which shall proceed out of thy bowels, and I will establish his kingdom.
2Sa 7:13. He shall build an house for my name, and I will stablish the throne of his kingdom for ever.

2Sa 7:16. And thine house and thy kingdom shall be established for ever before thee: thy throne shall be established for ever.

Psalm 89:3-4, 19-29, 34-37.
3. I have made a covenant with my chosen, I have sworn unto David my servant,
4. Thy seed will I establish for ever, and build up thy throne to all generations. Selah.

19. Then thou spakest in vision to thy holy one, and saidst, I have laid help upon one that is mighty; I have exalted one chosen out of the people.
20. I have found David my servant; with my holy oil have I anointed him:
21. With whom my hand shall be established: mine arm also shall strengthen him.

22. The enemy shall not exact upon him; nor the son of wickedness afflict him.
23. And I will beat down his foes before his face, and plague them that hate him.
24. But my faithfulness and my mercy shall be with him: and in my name shall his horn be exalted.
25. I will set his hand also in the sea, and his right hand in the rivers.
26. He shall cry unto me, Thou art my father, my God, and the rock of my salvation.
27. Also I will make him my firstborn, higher than the kings of the earth.
28. My mercy will I keep for him for evermore, and my covenant shall stand fast with him.
29. His seed also will I make to endure for ever, and his throne as the days of heaven.

34. My covenant will I not break, nor alter the thing that is gone out of my lips.
35. Once have I sworn by my holiness that I will not lie unto David.
36. His seed shall endure for ever, and his throne as the sun before me. Jesus Christ is the greater Son of David who has inherited His father's kingdom and will rule over it forever Isaiah. 9:6-7
6. For unto us a child is born, unto us a son is given: and the government shall be upon his shoulder: and his name shall be called Wonderful, Counsellor, The mighty God, The everlasting Father, The Prince of Peace.
7. Of the increase of his government and peace there shall be no end, upon the throne of David, and upon his kingdom, to order it, and to establish it with judgment and with justice from henceforth even for ever.

The zeal of the LORD of hosts will perform this.

Matthew 1:1
1. The book of the generation of Jesus Christ, the son of David, the son of Abraham.

Luke 1:32
32. He shall be great, and shall be called the Son of the Highest: and the Lord God shall give unto him the throne of his father David:

Jesus Christ is the King of kings who will come and establish an eternal kingdom, and the believers at Philadelphia were strengthened by being reminded of this fact. This present world, with its suffering and mockery and blasphemy and lies and unrequited unrighteousness, will soon pass, and then the humble believer will be exalted to rule and reign with Christ.

The term "the key of the house of David" is used in Isaiah 22:22 to refer to Eliakim, and it looks beyond him to the Messiah. Eliakim was a type of Christ.

HE THAT OPENETH AND NO MAN SHUTTETH,
HE THAT SHUTTETH AND NO MAN OPENETH

This is a statement that speaks to the OMNIPOTENCE of Christ. Remember I said during the pandemic HE was regaining CONTROL of His Church. He rules the heaven and the earth. He is in control of life and death. He has authority over the saved and unsaved. Christ is the HEAD OF THE CHURCH. With sovereign AUTHORITY over the church. Christ is the foundation of the church. In the words of S.J. Stone

The Church's one foundation
is Jesus Christ, her Lord;
she is his new creation
by water and the Word.
From heav'n he came and sought her
to be his holy bride;
with his own blood he bought her,
and for her life he died.

David Cloud wrote in "The Seven Churches of Revelation Then and Now", Philadelphia was a model church. Together with Smyrna, it is the only church that has no warning about sin and error and no call to repentance. Christ knows their works and condition (Rev. 3:8). He knows them intimately. He knows that they had a little strength. This means they had only a little strength. This was a weak, insignificant church, possibly small in numbers and certainly in resources, poor in worldly goods and of small account in the eyes of man. It was not wealthy and impressive. It was not comprised of those who were mighty in this world. Its leaders did not have impressive credentials. However, they had a love for one another and a love toward Christ that helped them to be a model church. Even though they had little strength, this church KEPT HIS WORD. No church can survive without the word of God. David said Psalm 119:11 Thy word have I hid in mine heart, that I might not sin against thee. During the time of John's exile on the Isle of Patmos, the church was being persecuted. But these faithful saints in Philadelphia NEVER DENIED THE NAME OF CHRIST. They held fast to their confession. They kept His word and did not deny His name. There was no room for compromising or conforming to any strange doctrine. It pleases Jesus when we hold up the standard. When we refuse to bow to any image that makes an attempt to exist alongside Him and share His Glory. Wherefore God hath exalted him, and given him a name which is above every name: That at the name of Jesus every knee should bow, of things in heaven, and things in earth; And that every tongue should confess that Jesus Christ is Lord, to the glory of God the Father (Philippians 2:9-11). Jesus said "Whosoever therefore shall confess me before men, him will I confess also before my Father which is in heaven. But whosoever shall deny me before men, him will I also deny before my Father which is in heaven". (Matthew 10:32-33). I admonish you to be not like this world, who would only accept Jesus as a "Good Man" or just "A Prophet". He is more than just a man and more than just a prophet. To minimize as such is to deny His Lordship, and His

Godness. To minimize Him as just some great person who walked the face of the earth and performed miracles, is to deny that He is the only begotten of the Father who in the beginning was with God, and was God and while He was in the form of God, thought it not robbery to be equal with God but made Himself of no reputation, and took upon him the form of a servant, and was made in the likeness of men: We can't deny him. If we deny him, we deny the work of the cross and His resurrection from the dead. To deny Jesus, is to make an attempt to erase the only means by which salvation from sin can be obtained.

Jesus closes this letter to the Philadelphia Church with a great assurance for the believer.

Rev 3:9 "And watch as I take those who call themselves true believers but are nothing of the kind, pretenders whose true membership is in the club of Satan--watch as I strip off their pretentions and they're forced to acknowledge it's you that I've loved. (MSG)

He promises to deal accordingly with those who proclaim to be believers with their words, but their hearts are far from it. The message translation calls them PRETENDERS. These are they who will arrive before the throne and be DISMISSED as workers of iniquity. Christ will say to them "I NEVER KNEW YOU." Standing on His Word and not denying Him but rather EXALTING HIM will result in Him performing His Word over your life and Exalting You.

Rev 3:10 "Because you kept my Word in passionate patience, I'll keep you safe in the time of testing that will be here soon, and all over the earth, every man, woman, and child put to the test.

Judgment will begin in the house of God. So what Christ is saying here is, if we continue to be a church that refuses to become worldly for the sake of swelling our numbers, if we stand firm on the statutes of holiness as we near the return of our savior. When judgment comes (time of testing) we will be kept safe from His wrath and be judged as righteous in His sight.

Rev 3:11 "I'm on my way; I'll be there soon. Keep a tight grip on what you have so no one distracts you and steals your crown. The CROWN OF RIGHTEOUSNESS which is our reward for running this race with patience.

Rev 3:12 "I'll make each conqueror a pillar in the sanctuary of my God, a permanent position of honor. Then I'll write names on you, the pillars: the Name of my God, the Name of God's City--the new Jerusalem coming down out of Heaven--and my new Name. So let us rejoice and be glad church. We will receive the MARK OF THE BLESSED not the MARK OF THE BEAST. Your faithfulness will have you branded with VICTORY. THE UNCOMPROMISED CHURCH, SHALL BE SEALED WITH VICTORY Rev 3:13 "Are your ears awake? Listen. Listen to the Wind Words, the Spirit blowing through the churches."

CHAPTER EIGHT
OPEN THE DOOR

And to the angel of the church in Laodicea say: These things says the true and certain witness, the head of God's new order: I have knowledge of your works, that you are not cold or warm: it would be better if you were cold or warm. So because you are not one thing or the other, I will have no more to do with you. For you say, I have wealth, and have got together goods and land, and have need of nothing; and you are not conscious of your sad and unhappy condition, that you are poor and blind and without clothing. If you are wise you will get from me gold tested by fire, so that you may have true wealth; and white robes to put on, so that your shame may not be seen; and oil for your eyes, so that you may see.
To all those who are dear to me, I give sharp words and punishment: then with all your heart have sorrow for your evil ways. See, I am waiting at the door and giving the sign; if my voice comes to any man's ears and he makes the door open, I will come in to him, and will take food with him and he with me. To him who overcomes I will give a place with me on my high seat, even as I overcame, and am seated with my Father on his high seat. He who has ears, let him give ear to what the Spirit says to the churches.
(Revelation 3:14-22)

This final church that receives a letter is the Church of Laodicea. Jesus, finding nothing good to say about this congregation, identifies Himself in a threefold manner. 1. The Amen, The Firm, The Trustworthy, The Surely. This identifies Christ as the firm, trusted and sure FOUNDATION of the church. He is the Christ, the son of the living God and upon that irrefutable truth (this rock) Christ has built His church, and the gates of hell will never prevail. These things say the Amen: Jesus is the Amen, the "so be it," the "it is done." As 2 Corinthians 1:20 says, For all the promises of God in Him are "Yes," and in Him "Amen." Jesus is "the personification and the affirmation of the truth of God."

2. The Faithful and True Witness: This is Jesus, and this was a contrast

to the Laodiceans, who will be shown to be neither faithful nor true.

3. Beginning of the creation of God: The idea behind the word for beginning [the ancient Greek word arche] is that of a "ruler, source, or origin," not of first in a sequential order. This verse does not teach that Jesus was the first being created, but that He is the ruler, source, and origin of all creation. It has the idea of first in prominence more than first in sequence.

These titles emphasize the Lord's faithfulness, sovereignty and power to bring all things to their proper completion (the "AMEN").

What we know about Laodicea is that during the time of this letter, it was a wealthy commercial center, and some of its goods were exported all over the world. "It has been noted that Laodicea prided itself on three things: FINANCIAL WEALTH, the TEXTILE INDUSTRY, and A POPULAR EYE-SALVE. They were also unfortunately known for their poor water supply. Their main water supply came on a six-mile aqueduct from the hot springs of Hierapolis. Because the water came from hot springs, it arrived un-appetizingly lukewarm. Too hot to be cold and too cold to be hot. There is nothing more horrible than tepid (lukewarm) water. Which means there is nothing more repugnant to Christ than a "tepid" church. It's painful to see that most of our churches are in this "lukewarm" condition. This UNENTHUSIASTIC, APATHETIC, UNINTERESTED mentality that has infiltrated the church, has crippled our potential to evangelize, witness and win souls to Christ. Allow me to quote Clarence

Larkin "Revival meetings are held, but instead of waiting on the Lord for power, evangelist and paid singers are hired and soul winning is made a business". Rev 3:16 You're stale. You're stagnant. You make me want to vomit. (msg) With all of our shouting and dancing. With all of our conferences, conventions and convocations, it is unfortunate that we have nauseated the spirit. Or in other words, GRIEVED THE SPIRIT. Ephesians 4:30 says Don't grieve God. Don't break his heart. His Holy Spirit, moving and breathing in you, is the most intimate part of your life, making you fit for himself. Don't take such a gift for granted.

Jesus threatens to SPIT THEM OUT, the same way they would spit out the tepid waters of their city.
    Because of their wealth, this church operated with a vain,

narcissistic, pleased with oneself, self-loving, in love with oneself, self-admiring, self-regarding, self-centered, egotistic, proud, arrogant, boastful, cocky spirit. Jesus says to them "you say you are rich" which shows that they were full of themselves, self-satisfied, self-congratulatory, complacent, haughty, vainglorious, peacockish, had an excessively high opinion of themselves, thought too highly of themselves, blew their own trumpet. It is impossible for the church to fulfill the great commission with that type of spirit.

    The statement "WE ARE RICH" automatically yet inadvertently makes MONEY THEIR GOD. It says the poor are beneath us. It says we are of a better class of people. It says we are of the elite and anyone not in our tax bracket really doesn't belong here. However, Jesus doesn't see them as rich. Even though they have earthly wealth, He identifies them as POOR. For too often, we have witnessed the miserable life of celebrities who seem to have it all. But they are the loneliest, most depressed people you'd ever meet. Rev 3:17 (msg) You brag, 'I'm rich, I've got it made, I need nothing from anyone,' oblivious that in fact you're a pitiful, blind beggar, threadbare and homeless. They had no idea how bad off they really were. Jesus challenges their god of wealth. Rev 3:18 (msg) "Here's what I want you to do: Buy your gold from me, gold that's been through the refiner's fire. Then you'll be rich. In other words, what you have will burn up if tested by the fire of the Holy Ghost. You've gained the world but lost your soul.

Because they were experiencing a measure of success in the textile industry, Laodicea was heavily into fabrics, which one would only have to imagine made them a materialistic people. Turning this church into a fashion show. Dressed up on the outside, but messed up on the inside. Jesus challenges their god of materialism and instructs them to change their garments. Rev 3:18 (msg) Buy your clothes from me, clothes designed in Heaven. You've gone around half-naked long enough. In other words, you're uncovered. Naked in the spirit. You have no ability to do warfare in the spirit because you're not dressed in the whole amor. You're lukewarmness has bittered the flow of your praise, so you wear a spirit of heaviness when you should have on a garment of praise. Laodicea also specialized in eye salve, which was used when the medicine needed to work directly in your eye to relieve or treat eye conditions. Eye ointments are used to treat conditions such as dry eyes or eye infections. Jesus addresses their spiritual blindness. Rev. 3:18 (msg) And buy medicine for your eyes from me so you can see, really see. In other words, there's something wrong with your eyes. You see yourself rich and well off, I see you as poor and in a perpetual state of want. You see yourself as dressed and attractive, I see you as naked and disrobed. You're not a church, you're a dark lit social club with an emphasis on the wrong thing. CLEAR YOUR FOCUS. Get your eyes checked. The devil has blinded you and made you delusional. CLEAR YOUR FOCUS. Although this letter is painful to the church. We have a silver lining. Although we are being rebuked with no commendation from the Lord in this Laodicean letter, Jesus still provides HOPE and COMFORT when He says, Rev 3:19 (kjv) As many as I love, I rebuke and chasten: be zealous therefore, and repent. The house I was raised in, I heard my father say things like "I whooped you because I love you" or "It hurt me more than it hurt you." To be honest, this always sounded oxymoronic to me until I had children of my own. I realized that they were behaving contrary to what my wife and I had deposited within them. God made a deposit of holiness in His Church when he breathed into us. Therefore, He has every right to expect us to live and to conduct ourselves as the vessels of holiness that he requires. The chastening is not because he hates us. The chastening is because he loves us and has an expectation of us to prosper and be in good health even as our soul would prosper. Chastening comes from the parent NOT BECAUSE THE PARENT DISLIKES THE CHILD but BECAUSE

THE PARENT IS DISAPPOINTED IN THE CHILD. This letter to the church shows a clear disappointment. But even with the feeling of disappointment, Jesus still proclaims his Love for us. BE ZEALOUS This word zealous means "to be hot." This is His last message to the church. He says, "Be zealous." Be hot. Get on fire for God. He is ordering this church to forsake its lukewarm state, and He says, "Repent." This church needs repentance more than all the others. For Him to say REPENT means He is willing to receive us unto Himself. He is still willing to SAVE US. The command for us to REPENT means there is still hope for the church. There is still hope for His Bride. Rev 3:20 (kjv) Behold, I stand at the door, and knock: if any man hear my voice, and open the door, I will come in to him, and will sup with him, and he with me. In other words, we've had

Jesus standing on the outside as if His presence wasn't a priority to the church. We can't function without His presence. If Jesus is not in the church, then IT IS NOT THE CHURCH. So, He stands at the door and knocks. Not because he can't open the door on His own, but because He is not the one to force Himself upon us. BEHOLD, I STAND AT THE DOOR, AND KNOCK: I AM close enough for you to let me in. You are far enough to backslide. If any man Hear my voice. To no other church does He make this statement. Laodicea is guilty of believing their own hype (hearing their own voice). But Jesus says HEAR MY VOICE and OPEN THE DOOR. We've closed Jesus out of His church long enough. Making us a church that has been devoid of miracles, signs and wonders. While He stands on the outside, we pretend like he is on the

inside which causes people to leave the same way they came. OPEN THE DOOR, Jesus is the lifeline to the church. We can't live without Him. OPEN THE DOOR, He wants to take residence in us. John 15:7 (kjv) If ye abide in me, and my words abide in you, ye shall ask what ye will, and it shall be done unto you. OPEN THE DOOR, He wants to sup with us and wants us to sup with Him. Jesus desires to dine with His church. Jesus desires to be in Fellowship with us. This is a call to conversion, communion, and covenant.
Rev 3:21 (kjv) To him that overcometh will I grant to sit with me in my throne, even as I also overcame, and am set down with my Father in his throne. Opening the door will make us OVERCOMERS. Opening the door will make us JOINT HEIRS with Jesus Christ. We shall REIGN with Him. FOREVER.

Rev 3:22 (kjv) He that hath an ear, let him hear what the Spirit saith unto the churches.

CHAPTER NINE
IN CONCLUSION
Let all things be done
DECENTLY AND IN ORDER.
1 Corinthians 14:40

While we are indeed living in the last days. We still have today to change and to make every attempt to please the father. It is my prayer that we come to the realization of the fact that we as the church of Jesus Christ must prioritize being in order. Serving Him with sincerity and fullness of heart. It is also my prayer that reading this book has opened our eyes to the possible state of the church in our modern years. I am by no means the professional churchman, as I have seen myself in all seven of these churches that Our Lord has addressed. If you see yourself, I suggest you RESPOND to His announcement. RECALIBRATE your LOVE for Him. RECOMMIT your LIFE to Him. RESIST the devil. REFRAIN from the Jezebel spirit. RETURN from your dead state. REMAIN in fellowship with the saints. And REPENT for being out of order.

Ecclesiastes 1:9 says The thing that hath been, it is that which shall be; and that which is done is that which shall be done: and there is no new thing under the sun.
I wish to thank EVERY THEOLOGIAN whose works I have had the pleasure of studying in order to write this book.
Clarence Larkin
J. Vernon McGee,
C.I. Scofield,
David Guzik
David Cloud
Dr. Richard Booker

The Company of Scholars whose work makes up The Preachers Outline and Sermon Bible.

Living with your work has enabled me to articulate my heart in this body of work that I present to the Kingdom and offer to the Lord as my contribution to HIS CHURCH.
Four of the greatest preachers I've ever heard have encouraged me to be the best preaching representative of the kingdom I can possibly be. Rev. Dr. Jeremiah Fennell, Archbishop Eric R. Figueroa, Sr, Bishop Gerald G. Seabrooks & Apostle Wilbur L. Jones, Sr. Thank you for every measure of oil I have received from you. Thank you for being in my life. I hope to have made you proud.

I pray that when our Lord returns, He will find us as a church without a spot or wrinkle. That he would immediately

see His blood on us so that eternal damnation would pass over us. I pray that He will ORDER our steps as ORDER is restored in HIS CHURCH. LET THERE BE ORDER IN THE CHURCH.
Amen

Made in the USA
Middletown, DE
19 November 2024

64950040R00060